Behavior in Living Things

Michael Bright

Chicago, Illinois

www.capstonepub.com
Visit our website to find out more information about Heinemann-Raintree books.

To order:

☎ Phone 888-454-2279
💻 Visit www.capstonepub.com
to browse our catalog and order online.

© 2012 Raintree
an imprint of Capstone Global Library, LLC
Chicago, Illinois

Edited by Andrew Farrow, Adrian Vigliano, and Diyan Leake
Designed by Victoria Allen
Picture research by Elizabeth Alexander
Illustrations by Oxford Designers & Illustrators
Originated by Capstone Global Library Ltd

Library of Congress Cataloging-in-Publication Data
Bright, Michael.

Behavior in living things / Michael Bright.

p. cm.—(The web of life)

Includes bibliographical references and index.

ISBN 978-1-4109-4398-9 (hb (freestyle))—ISBN 978-1-4109-4405-4 (pb (freestyle)) 1. Animal behavior—Juvenile literature. 2. Animal psychology—Juvenile literature. I. Title.

QL751.5.B747 2012

591.5—dc23   2011017728

Image Credits

Alamy: Gallo Images, cover, INTERFOTO, 18, Janine Wiede, 41, Nature Picture Library, 21 bottom, Phil Degginger, 15; Biosphoto: GUNTHER MICHEL, 29;Getty Images: Clive Bromhall/Oxford Scientific, 28 bottom, Fuse, 28 middle, Martin Harvey, 27; iStockphoto: Andy Gehrig, 24, Sandeep Subba, 36, Sharon Dominick, 35 top; Minden Pictures: Cyril Ruoso, 12, Jim Brandenburg, 25; Nature Picture Library: Miles Barton, 31; Oxford University: Behavioural Ecology Research Group, Oxford University, 17; Photolibrary: AlaskaStock, 40; Photoshot: ANDY ROUSE, 8; Reuters Pictures: STR, 11; Robert Harding: Tom Walmsley, 6; Science Source: ASTIER, 38; Shutterstock: Cathy Keifer, 33, cbpix, 21 top, CREATISTA, 39, Elena Elisseeva, 35 bottom, Graeme Dawes, 37, János Németh, 22, Ken Griffiths, 23, Mogens Trolle, 9, Monkey Business Images, 5, Neale Cousland, 13, Pang Chee Seng Philip, 19, Peter Kirillov, 10, uzuri, 28 top, worldclassphoto, 14 top, Yann hubert, 30; SuperStock: Biosphoto, 16, Jim Watt, 4, Norbert Wu, 14 bottom

Every effort has been made to contact copyright holders of material reproduced in this book. Any omissions will be rectified in subsequent printings if notice is given to the publisher.

Disclaimer
All the internet addresses (URLs) given in this book were valid at the time of going to press. However, due to the dynamic nature of the internet, some addresses may have changed, or sites may have changed or ceased to exist since publication. While the author and publisher regret any inconvenience this may cause readers, no responsibility for any such changes can be accepted by either the author or the publisher.

Contents

Some words appear in the text in bold, **like this**. You can find out what they mean by looking in the glossary.

What Is Behavior?

Behavior is something we all do. All plants and animals show behavior, too—even tiny **bacteria**. Behavior can be a simple reflex action, such as pulling your hand away from a hot stove. It can also be more complex behavior, such as a humpback whale singing in the ocean.

Scientists study behavior because they want to understand how living **organisms** behave and interact. One of these scientists was Nobel Prize-winning Dutch **biologist** Nikolaas Tinbergen (1907–1988). He suggested that, when we look at any behavior, we should ask ourselves the four basic questions below:

Cause	What is the **stimulus** that causes the response, and has learning **modified** (changed) it? A stimulus is something that influences an activity or causes an organism to respond.
Development	What early experiences are necessary for the behavior to appear and how does it change with age?
Evolution	How does the behavior of one **species** compare with that of a related species, and how might it have **evolved**?
Function	How does the behavior influence the animal's chance of survival and its ability to reproduce?

When a great white shark chases seals, its feeding behavior can be spectacular.

The answers to these four questions can help you discover the different things that might influence why you behave, or why a plant or animal behaves, in a particular way. Remembering them is as easy as learning your ABCs. Remember A-B-C-D-E-F— **A**bout **B**ehavior: **C**ause, **D**evelopment, **E**volution, and **F**unction.

Why do you eat?

You probably haven't thought too much about why you eat, but it's a behavior we all do every day. So, let's ask Tinbergen's questions about our own eating behaviors.

Cause	What stimulates you to eat? Do you eat because it is breakfast, lunch, or dinner time? Do you eat because you are hungry? Now think again: when you smell a baking doughnut, do you eat it because you are hungry?
Development	How did you eat just after you were born? How have your eating habits changed as you have grown older?
Evolution	How does the way you eat compare, say, to a chimpanzee? Is there anything we do when eating that might indicate that humans and chimpanzees are in any way related (see page 26)?
Function	How do you think eating makes it possible for you to survive?

Human feeding behavior can follow a fixed pattern and involve certain **rituals**. Rituals are things we do over and over again in an established routine. What human feeding rituals can you think of?

Hard-wired, or Acquired?

Behavior can be broadly divided into "instinctive behavior" and "learned behavior."

Instinct

Some behavior is instinctive. It is inborn, or exits from birth. The instructions for the behavior are passed from parents to offspring in the **genes**. They cause an animal to react automatically to a **stimulus**. For example, when sea turtle hatchlings emerge from their underground nests in the sand, they automatically head toward the sea. Scientists believe the stimulus to be the brightness of the sky over the sea in front of them and the darkness of the land behind the nest. They can see the difference even in starlight at night.

As the hatchlings have only just emerged from their eggs, there has been no opportunity for them to learn anything from their parents. So moving toward light must be an instinctive behavior.

Learning

Other behavior is learned. It can be learned from parents, or maybe from an animal's own experience. An animal can **modify** this behavior and change its response to a stimulus. For example, young chimpanzees learn how to crack nuts or to fish with sticks for termites and ants by watching their mother, who already has these skills. The young chimpanzees get better with practice.

Sea turtle hatchlings head instinctively in the direction of the sea.

Which way?

It is sometimes difficult to work out which behavior is instinctive and which is learned. For example, do **migrating** birds instinctively know which direction to fly, or do they learn? Dutch biologist Albert Perdeck carried out an experiment to find out.

Each winter, European starlings migrate from the eastern Baltic to northern France. They stop off briefly to refuel in the Netherlands. Perdeck captured some birds and took them to Switzerland. He then released them. First the young starlings flew away, followed by the older ones. When the birds were caught again, all of the younger birds were found to have continued heading southwest, as before. They ended up in Spain and southern France, and not where they should have been. However, the older birds adjusted their course. They arrived at their intended destination in northern France.

Perdeck had shown that young starlings inherit the tendency to **orient** in a given direction (instinct). However, the experiences they gain as they grow older enable them to find their way more accurately (learning).

Here you can see the effect Albert Perdeck's experiment had on the young starlings. They continued to head southwest and ended up far from their usual winter homes.

N

Key
— Adults' migration
— Juveniles' migration
-- Normal migration route
▨ Normal winter area

| 0 | | 500 | | 1000 km |

| 0 | 200 | 400 | 600 miles |

UK

THE NETHERLANDS

SWITZERLAND

FRANCE

SPAIN

Instinct: Fight or Flight

In order to survive an attack in the wild, animals have automatic responses during which they either fight or flee.

Red alert

A house cat is out walking when a dog suddenly confronts it. The cat's heartbeat accelerates quickly so oxygen-rich blood is pumped to its muscles. Its hair stands on end to make it look bigger. The pupils in its eyes **dilate** so it can see everything it needs to. All its senses are on "red-alert."

The reaction is automatic. The cat's entire body is ready to fight the dog or to run away. But it cannot keep up the flight or fight response for long. It would use up too much energy and maybe even damage its body. So it is only used briefly in order to confront danger or flee from it.

Other animals have different fight-or-flight reactions. A zebra about to be attacked by a lion explodes into life. If it stopped to think what to do, it would be caught and killed. In a fraction of a second, the zebra is running for its life. If cornered, however, it lashes out, kicking at the lion with its hind legs and razor-sharp hooves.

A zebra's first reaction is to flee, but, if cornered, it fights.

What's the message?

If a springbok spots a **predator** out hunting, it behaves quite unexpectedly. Instead of running away immediately, like the zebra, it leaps straight up into the air with stiff legs and all four feet off the ground. This flight behavior is known as "stotting" or "pronking." Why do you think the springbok behaves in this way?

- Is it an alarm signal—a way of warning other springbok that a predator is nearby?

- Is it a way to attract the predator to itself and, so, away from the rest of the herd—a self-sacrificing behavior known as altruism?

- When several springbok leap at different times, is it a way to confuse the predator so it cannot focus on one individual?

- Is it a way to tell the predator that the springbok is a very healthy animal and so the predator should not bother chasing it?

At one time or another, scientists have offered all of these explanations. Which one do you think is best? Whatever the answer, the behavior seems to work because the predator usually stops hunting the springbok.

The springbok's peculiar stiff-legged leaping sends a message to its predators.

Nature School

Animals learn from parents, from other animals of their own kind, and from their own experiences. Scientists have identified many different types of learning. Here are just a few examples of learned behavior:

Go for a walk?

You may have noticed that your dog runs to the front door as soon as you pick up its leash to go for a walk. This behavior is known as conditioning. The response becomes automatic, but the behavior is learned. The dog learns to associate the leash with going for a walk.

Prairie dogs, living near trails used regularly by people, learn not to give alarm calls when people walk by. This is a form of learning called **habituation**.

Winter store

A jay buries acorns in the forest in autumn. It returns to exactly the same place to recover them in winter. This is called spatial learning. The jay remembers the landmarks close to where it buried the acorns.

Yuck!

When a toad catches a millipede, protected by foul-tasting poisons, it spits it out. The toad quickly learns that the millipede is not good to eat. This is called trial-and-error learning.

When under attack, a bombardier beetle sprays out a boiling hot, poisonous fluid (see below). This distracts the **predator**, giving the beetle time to spread its wings and fly away.

Tricking digger wasps

Scientists carried out a fascinating experiment involving spatial learning. A female digger wasp dug a nest in the ground. The entrance was well hidden. Inside the nest were the wasp's offspring. She left the nest regularly to find food for them. As she flew out, she circled the surrounding area for a few seconds. Then, she darted off to go hunting.

The scientists believed that she was memorizing the landmarks around the nest so she would be able to find it again on her return. To check whether their theory was correct, the scientists moved the landmarks around a little while she was gone.

Imagine the wasp's confusion when she returned to find that her nest entrance was not where the landmarks indicated it should have been. Even with a brain the size of a pinhead, a wasp learns and remembers the positions of landmarks.

The macaques that wash potatoes

Sometimes animals surprise scientists with their cleverness. They invent new behaviors and then learn these new behaviors from one another. A group of macaques (a type of monkey) on a tiny island in Japan did exactly this.

Researchers wanted to draw the macaques out into the open so they could study their behavior. So they regularly scattered sweet potatoes on a beach. Inevitably, the potatoes were covered in sand. One monkey—a female called Imo—figured out that washing the potatoes in a nearby stream was a way to clean off the sand. Other monkeys, especially those of her own age, watched and learned by **imitation** (copying) to do the same thing.

Imo then found that a potato tasted better if she washed it in seawater. She would take a bite, dip the potato in the water, and take another bite. The potato was being seasoned with salt from the sea. Soon, 15 of the 19 youngsters in the group had copied her example, but only 2 of the 11 (mostly male) adults.

Why do you think there was this difference between the age groups? The answer is that older male monkeys tend to keep apart from younger ones, who were with Imo.

Eventually, the young potato-washing monkeys grew up and had babies of their own. Most of these babies acquired the skill of potato washing. They learned the behavior from their mothers.

Japanese macaques learn from each other to wash sweet potatoes before eating them.

WHAT IT MEANS FOR US

Watching these macaques was one of the first times that scientists had observed and described new behavior (invention) passing through a population. It was not only passed among group members (imitation), but also from one generation to the next.

Imo and the wheat grain

Imo turned out to be exceptionally bright. When the researchers put wheat grains on the beach for the group to eat, she grabbed a handful of wheat and sand and threw it on to the water. The sand sank, but the wheat floated to the surface. She could then pick up the grains without the sand.

It took a little longer for this behavior to be copied by the others. This is because monkeys, like many other animals, will not usually let go of food once they take hold of it.

Japanese macaques have also learned that hot springs keep them warm in winter, but only **dominant** animals and those that groom them are allowed in.

WORD BANK
imitation   the act of copying the behavior of others
dominant   having the most influence or control

Mimicry

Mimicry is the **resemblance** of one animal to another so that one might be confused for the other. Some animals mimic other animals by copying their physical appearance. For example, hover flies get protection from predators by having the same kinds of black-and-yellow markings as wasps and hornets, which the predators would not attack. Other animals duplicate behavior and appearance. One of the most clever mimics is an octopus.

The mimic octopus

Mimicry can help protect an animal. Many **species** of octopus are able to match the color of their surroundings. They camouflage themselves as rocks, corals, or part of the ocean floor to avoid being seen by predators. The mimic octopus in Indonesian waters has gone a stage further. It mimics the shape, color, texture, and behavior of other sea creatures – especially dangerous ones.

The mimic octopus is so clever it can recognize the predator that is threatening it. The octopus then decides which animal to mimic in order to get away.

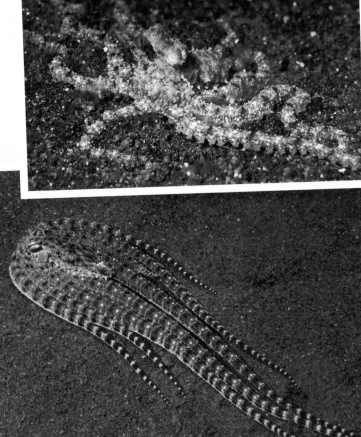

The mimic octopus above is using the pattern on its tentacles to blend in with the sandy background on the sea floor. The octopus on the right is **imitating** a venomous sole fish.

- When attacked by a damselfish, the mimic octopus turns black and yellow. It holds six of its arms against its body and waves the other two forward and backward. It resembles a banded sea snake, a species that eats damselfish.

- To mimic a poisonous sole fish, the mimic octopus pulls in its arms and flattens its body. Using a sort of jet propulsion, it swims away with the **undulating** motion of a flatfish.

- By resting on the ocean floor with its arms curved above its body, the mimic octopus looks like a sea anemone with waving, stinging tentacles.

- Hovering just above the ocean floor with its arms spread wide, the octopus mimics the venomous lionfish.

Fatal fireflies

Fireflies are flying beetles that can give off light to attract mates and **prey**. Some female *Photuris* fireflies mimic the lights of female *Photinus* fireflies. When the male *Photinus* firefly arrives, the female *Photuris* eats him. The female does this to get an easy meal and to get chemicals that protect her from jumping spiders. The female *Photuris* firefly cannot make these chemicals herself.

The male *Photinus*, or big dipper firefly, is lured to his death by females of another species.

Do Animals Think?

When the English naturalist Charles Darwin (1809–1882) was alive, it was generally believed that humans were unique in being intelligent. People thought that animals' lives were controlled entirely by instinct. Darwin, however, knew differently. He wrote that "animals possess some power of reasoning." Since then, researchers have discovered that animals show more signs of intelligent behavior than even Darwin could have imagined.

Mirror test

Are animals aware of themselves? When you look in a mirror, you see yourself. You know that it is you. If you have dirt on your face, you can remove it by looking in the mirror. Researchers have used this everyday human behavior to test whether animals are self-aware. They put two black dots on an animal's face. If it looks at itself in the mirror and tries to remove the spots, the animal shows that it has recognized the image in the mirror as itself.

At first, only the great apes—gorillas, chimpanzees, bonobos, orangutans, and humans—passed this test. As more animals were tested, more appeared to recognize "self." They included rhesus macaques, bottlenose dolphins, orcas (killer whales), elephants, and European magpies. There is a problem with these tests, however. How can we test animals that usually use senses other than sight?

Animals that recognize "self" include rhesus macaques, bottlenose dolphins, orcas, elephants, and European magpies.

Betty the crow makes a bent hook from an aluminium strip to pull a bucket of food up a tube.

Clever bird

Scientists at Oxford University had a big surprise when a New Caledonian crow called Betty, a subject of a laboratory study, showed extraordinary skills.

Many animals are known to use tools, but Betty went a step further. She wanted to get at food that was just out of reach in a bucket at the bottom of a tube. She took a straight piece of wire and bent it into a hook shape. Then she lowered it into the tube and pulled up the bucket to get the food.

Betty could not have learned this behavior from other birds. She solved the problem by doing something she had never done before. She was being creative. She identified the challenge, selected a raw material, worked out the right shape needed, made a tool, and got the food.

Animal Emotions: Real or Imagined?

When a baby gorilla dies, the mother carries the body for several days. Is she **mourning**? If elephants see an elephant corpse or skeleton, they sniff the bones with their trunks and gently touch the body with the soles of their feet. What are they thinking? Nonhuman animals respond to pain and show signs of fear. Are they as aware of these things as we are? Do they have a similar capacity for emotions (feelings) as humans? Questions like these are a challenge for those studying animal behavior.

Elephants behave strangely, almost **mystically**, when confronted with the remains of other elephants.

Moody dogs

A study of pet dogs reveals that, just like people, there are **optimists** and **pessimists** among them. In the experiment, each dog was held behind a screen. A food bowl was put out on the other side of the screen. If the bowl was placed on one side of the room, it contained a delicious treat. If it was placed on the other side, it had nothing in it.

The dogs quickly learned which side meant a treat and raced to the bowl. If the bowl was placed on the non-treat side, the dogs would lie down, look around, or even sigh.

Then the bowl was placed in new positions around the room. Some dogs ran to check the bowl. These were the optimists. Others were less interested. They were called the pessimists.

Emotional animals

Emotions may tell animals how dangerous their world is or how easy it is to find food or other resources. Their emotions might reflect not only the experiences they have had in the past, but also might guide the choices that they make in the future.

The bloodhound might look sad, but there's a good chance that this dog is actually an optimist.

Half empty or half full?

One way to begin to understand animal emotions is to look at choices animals make in their everyday lives. An animal that is regularly threatened by **predators** might develop a negative emotion, such as **anxiety**. It is a pessimist. It is more cautious. It suspects that each rustle in the grass is a predator. In contrast, an animal that has easy access to food has a more positive "attitude." It is an optimist. It interprets a rustle in the grass as potential **prey**.

WORD BANK
optimist   someone who usually expects the best to happen in any situation
pessimist   someone who usually expects the worst to happen in any situation

Communication

Animals communicate in many ways. Birds and whales sing, and frogs croak. Fiddler crabs wave their claws. Squid change the color patterns on their skin. Honeybees dance. Elephant knife fish talk to each other using electricity. Hippopotamuses communicate with their manure.

Communication has many uses. It is used to bring males and females together during **courtship**. It can declare that a **territory** is occupied. It can ensure that all the animals in a hunting pack are working together. It can settle a battle between two male animals. It can warn of danger. It can also be used to indicate where food might be found. Animals that communicate the most tend to be those that live together. Why do you think this might be?

False danger warning

Most communication is between animals of the same **species**. However, sometimes it can be between members of different species. Alarm calls are an example. Some animals use these alarm calls to cheat. In South America, multi-species flocks of antbirds feed on the insects that are disturbed by the marching columns of army ants.

However, two species of antbird trick the other birds. When another type of antbird goes to catch an escaping insect, the trickster antbird gives an alarm call. The first bird is fooled into thinking that danger is near. It drops the insect and flies away. The trickster then flies down and catches the insect for itself.

Body language

One form of communication is **body language**. When a dog wags its tail, it is happy. When a cat arches its back, it is showing **aggression**. When an elephant sticks out its ears, it is very angry. When a male baboon yawns, it is saying, "I'm the boss around here." Can you think of examples of your own body language (see pages 38–41)?

WHAT IT MEANS FOR US

Gray reef sharks use body language to warn other sharks, and even people, to keep away. They arch their backs, point their pectoral fins down, raise their snouts and swim stiffly. Anyone who fails to heed the warning is attacked. So, if you see a shark behaving in this way, back away slowly, and leave the water as soon as you can.

In India, chital deer live with hanuman langurs. The monkeys up in the trees spot tigers approaching and give an alarm call that warns the deer. The deer detect the sounds and smells of hidden tigers and warn the langurs.

Courtship and Competition

Many animals that live alone tend to avoid others of their own species. One reason is that they are competing for the same food and living space. This could be a problem at mating time, so these animals have developed elaborate **courtship rituals** to help them find a mate. For some spiders, it can mean the difference between life and death. The male nursery web spider pacifies the female by catching a fly, wrapping it in silk, and presenting it to her as a gift. He also pretends to be dead so she will not attack him. As soon
as her fangs are safely in the gift of food, he springs into life and mates with her. Then, he leaves quickly before she can catch him.

Competition between males

Some males have to fight for the right to mate with females. In red deer **society**, the "rut" separates the men from the boys. During the rut, the strongest stags first have roaring competitions. If they still seem to be equal, they size each other up by walking alongside each other. If that fails to impress, and one stag does not back down, they fight. They lock antlers and push and pull, until one defeats the other. The winner has access to several hinds (female deer).

Red deer square up to each other for the right to mate.

Female choice

Female animals often choose the fittest males, so their offspring will be strong and healthy, too. Therefore, males need to impress females. One of the most hard-working males is probably the satin bowerbird of Australia. He builds an avenue of twigs, known as a bower. He decorates it with any objects he can find that are colored blue—flowers, feathers, and berries. He even collects objects that are not normally found in nature, for example, ballpoint pens or even shotgun cartridges!

When a female appears, the male bowerbird dances on the stage in front of his bower. If she is impressed by his building skills and the energy of his dance, she mates with him. But, the bower is not a nest. The female builds her nest elsewhere and brings up her **brood** (young) alone.

Will the blue objects this male bowerbird has gathered be good enough to attract a female?

WORD BANK
ritual   pattern of behavior performed regularly in a set manner
society   social or communal group of individuals that are dependent on one another

Living Together

Some animals live together in groups. They are known as social animals. Wolves, wild dogs, and lions are social animals, as are honeybees, ants, and termites. In order to live peacefully alongside each other, social animals communicate frequently and have rules to prevent fights from breaking out. Wolves, for example, have an entire language of body postures that helps prevent aggression.

Pecking order

In many social animal groups, each individual has its place in society. In wolf society, it was once thought that the pack was led by "alpha wolves" who fought their way to the top. This is now believed to be wrong. The parents lead the pack. They are the oldest, and probably the wisest, wolves. Their offspring make up the rest of the pack. The younger wolves are more **passive** and, therefore, **submissive** to their parents. If they were not, then fights would break out. Fights waste energy and could cause serious injury, or even death.

Wolf talk

An **assertive** wolf stands tall with its tail horizontal. More passive wolves show their submission by walking low to the ground, with ears and tail turned down. They may lick the assertive wolf's face. A passive wolf might also lie on the ground and let the more **dominant** animal inspect it. However, before and after a hunt, wolves all howl together. In this way they can check that all are present and healthy. They also howl to warn neighboring packs to stay away.

A passive individual in the wolf pack shows submissive behavior to a more assertive individual, probably a parent, one of the pack's leaders.

Cooperative hunting

Generally the wolf pack hunts as a team. The extended family helps parents to catch food for any cubs. They rely on **stamina** to wear down their **prey**. They like to keep the prey running until it is too weak to put up a fight. If the prey stops, the wolves eventually lose interest. If it starts to run, they renew the chase. Working together they can chase down prey as large as moose, deer, and caribou. Each of these prey animals is much larger than an individual wolf.

By working together, wolves can bring down prey much larger than themselves.

WORD BANK
passive   inactive, submissive, or not resisting
assertive   bold or confident

The Chimpanzees of Gombe

In 1960, British **zoologist** Jane Goodall started to research the behavior of the chimpanzees in Gombe Stream National Park in Tanzania, Africa.

When she first arrived in Gombe, Goodall had to get the chimpanzees to accept her. She followed the group everywhere. By seeing her every day, the chimpanzees got used to her being there. In other words, they had become **habituated** (see page 10).

Jane Goodall's work with chimpanzees was in Gombe, beside Lake Victoria in the Great African Rift Valley. This region is also thought to be the birthplace of another **primate**—humans.

New discoveries

Very quickly, Goodall made some remarkable discoveries.

- First, she found the chimpanzees eating meat and later watched them hunt monkeys, bush pigs, and other small **mammals**. Until then, chimpanzees were thought to be **vegetarians**.

- Not long afterward, she found that the chimpanzees were using grass stems to "fish" for termites in termite mounds. They were making simple tools. Until that discovery, it was thought that only humans were toolmakers.

- A few years later, Goodall observed chimpanzees stealing, killing, and eating young chimpanzees. They had turned to **infanticide** and **cannibalism**. It was the first time this behavior had been seen in chimpanzees.

This chimpanzee learned from its mother how to "fish" for termites.

Toolmakers

To fish for termites, the chimpanzee takes a leafy stem and strips off the leaves. The stem is pushed into holes in the termite mound. The soldier termites grab the twig and are pulled out of their nest. The chimpanzee picks them off with his lips and chews them up. Young male and female chimpanzees behave differently. Young females learn earlier and spend more time fishing with their mothers. Males tend to play more. Why do you think this is? Are they practicing for later life?

When the youngsters grow up and become parents themselves, female chimpanzees will need to eat more termites. They will have babies to look after and will have no time to hunt meat, like the males. Males play more and fish less when they are young because they need to develop the fighting and hunting skills that they will need when grown up.

Call	Emotion
"Wraa"	Fear
"Huu"	Puzzled
Food grunt or food "aaa" call	Enjoying Food
Crying or whimpering	Distress
Arrival pant-hoot	Excitement

Chimp-talk

Chimpanzees communicate in a variety of ways, including a **body language** of postures and facial expressions. They also call with screams, barks, grunts, and hoots. At least one call—the very loud pant-hoot—is unique to individual chimpanzees, so they can tell who is calling, even if they cannot see the caller.

Making faces

Chimpanzees have many facial expressions. When the teeth show and the lips are pulled back vertically, it's an angry face (right). The pout face, with the lip puckered as if giving a kiss, indicates submission (below). The play face is one with mouth slightly open. This face indicates all is calm (below right).

There is no mistaking an angry chimpanzee. His face, body language, and the calls he makes indicate **aggression**.

Friendly chimpanzees

Apart from the occasional power struggle between **dominant** males, chimpanzees generally get along well together. They laugh at playtime, groom one another, touch hands, and enjoy tickling. Close bonds develop between family members and group members that last an entire lifetime. One teenager was even seen to "adopt" an orphan. However, chimpanzees also have a very dangerous side.

Chimpanzee hunters

When the Gombe chimpanzees go hunting, they are well organized. When they hunt colobus monkeys, two or three chimpanzees climb silently into the trees ahead of the monkey group and block any exits. Two flankers block any escape from the sides. When all the chimpanzees are in place, the catcher quickly climbs up the tree in which the colobus monkeys are hiding and grabs one. The monkey is torn apart and the pieces shared among the hunting team.

WHAT IT MEANS FOR US

Jane Goodall discovered that chimpanzees are often at war with their neighbors. Bands of chimpanzees gang up on a neighboring group and kill them. In fact, while Jane was studying the Gombe chimpanzees, there was a four-year war between two groups. It ended with one group wiping out the other. It was the first record of long-term warfare in groups of nonhuman primates.

Chimpanzees are our nearest living relatives, and we share a common prehistoric ancestor. So, what do you think this behavior means for us? Does **evolution** (see page 4) apply here? Could it mean that humans, like chimpanzees, have a natural tendency to start wars?

The work continues

Jane Goodall now spends most of her time working for the conservation of chimpanzees. However, the fieldwork that she started continues at the Gombe Stream Research Center, which is part of the Jane Goodall Institute. You can read more about this work at: www.janegoodall.org.

Jane Goodall is seen here interacting with a Gombe chimpanzee.

Tool Use

Chimpanzees and crows are not the only nonhuman animals to make and use tools. A surprising number of animals, and even insects, also use tools.

Herons fishing

When green herons go fishing, they deliberately and carefully place **bait** in the form of insects, feathers, and thin twigs on the surface of the water. This baiting behavior lures fish up to the surface, and the herons then catch the fish more easily.

Dolphin protection

A female bottlenose dolphin in Western Australia was seen with a piece of marine sponge draped over her beak. Later observations revealed that she had ripped the sponge from the ocean floor and then used it, like a protective glove, to help prevent her beak being stung by stonefish. The stonefish lives on the ocean floor and is protected by sharp, venomous spines. The dolphin roots about on the ocean floor looking for fish, and a sting from a stonefish would be very painful. Now, several other dolphins have been observed doing the same thing. Young dolphins, mostly daughters, copy the **foraging** behavior from their mothers.

Dolphins use sponges to protect their beaks from venomous fish.

Crows use traffic lights

In Japan, carrion crows watch vehicles at pedestrian traffic lights. When the lights turn red, the cars stop, the people cross, and the crows place walnuts (collected from nearby trees) on to the road. When the lights turn green, the crows fly up, and the cars run over the walnuts and crack them. When the lights turn red again, the crows join the pedestrians on the crosswalk and pick up the pieces of crushed nut.

Tool-bug

Perhaps the most surprising tool user is the Costa Rican assassin bug. It is an **invertebrate** with the tiniest of brains, but it is clever enough to use a tool. The bug stakes out a termite nest and captures a worker termite. It sucks out all of the termite's body juices. It then takes the **exoskeleton** (hard outer skin) and dangles it like a fishing lure. Termites are neat insects, so another worker comes along to clear away the dead body—but it gets more than it bargained for. The assassin bug drops the dead skin and grabs the undertaker termite.

The Japanese crow waits on the wires for traffic to crack the walnuts it has dropped in the road.

Hug a Tree

Plants respond to changes in the **environment**. Some plant behavior is easy to see. For example, plants grow toward or away from light. This is called phototropism. But it may come as a surprise to learn that plants communicate with other plants, and even plant-eating animals—and some actually move to catch food. In fact, plants behave in similar ways to animals.

Danger: thorn attack

In the southern United States, a vine-like plant in the bean family moves unusually fast. When disturbed, its leaflets fold up rapidly. The sudden movement is thought to scare away small plant eaters, such as insects, as their natural reaction is to flee from something that moves unexpectedly. However, larger plant eaters, such as slugs and **mammals**, are not so easily frightened. Instead, they are suddenly exposed to the sharp thorns on the leaf stems, and this scares them away.

Leaves of the Schrankia vine fold up to reveal sharp thorns.

leaflet

thorns

leaflet — thorns

thorns

It's raining, it's pouring

In the rainforests of Panama, the tropical liana plant moves its leaves for a different reason. It lowers its leaves in response to heavy rain (but not to light rain or insects landing). In this way, the leaves shed water and dry more quickly.

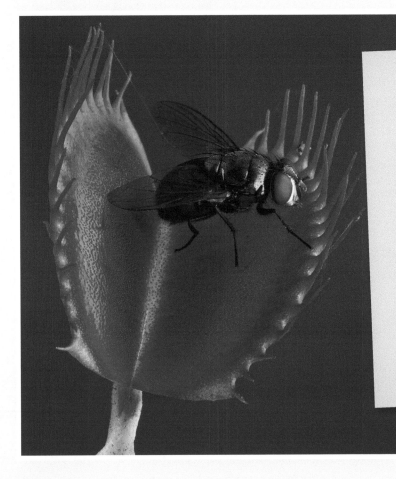

Flytrap

The Venus flytrap plant moves its leaves to catch flies for food. If a fly touches two tiny trigger hairs on a leaf surface, or touches the same hair twice, the leaf closes. The struggles of the trapped insect cause the plant to produce **enzymes** that digest its **prey**. This enables the plant to live in areas where **nutrients** are scarce, such as bogs.

Plant talk

In an experiment at the University of California, researchers clipped the leaves of sagebrush plants to mimic insect damage. The sagebrush sent out a chemical SOS signal that floated through the air and was picked up by tobacco plants near by. The tobacco plants responded by producing chemicals that made their leaves taste bad. Grasshoppers and caterpillars left them alone and moved to tobacco plants that were farther away and had not received the airborn signal. The resesearchers demonstrated that one plant can send a message to another.

WORD BANK
enzyme special chemical (protein) that helps chemical changes take place in living organisms
nutrient chemical an organism needs to live and grow

Pets and Farm Animals

Many animals have adapted to live as pets and as farm animals. For example, dogs have adapted to live and eat alongside people, but they still show signs of their wild ancestry. Man's best friend is actually a **domesticated** grey wolf (see pages 24–25).

Puppy love

Puppies demonstrate the same behavior as wolf cubs do from the moment they are born. A mother dog finds a hidden place to give birth, somewhere away from the noise and bustle of everyday life. From about the fifth week after birth, the pups play games that help them relate to other dogs. They have pretend fights. These games establish which pups are **assertive** and which are passive.

Assertive puppies, for example, will pick fights with more passive individuals. If a third puppy joins the fight, it will usually take the side of the more **dominant** puppy. Their mother disciplines them by staring at them, just as mother wolves do. She reprimands them with growls.

Puppies sometimes beg from an adult dog by licking its face. The adult might **regurgitate** food, just like wolves do. It is an instinctive response. The adult automatically brings up the food. It has little control over this behavior.

Big difference

Domestic dogs that have become **feral** may form packs (see page 25). Sometimes they will then hunt livestock, such as calves, sheep, goats, foals, and chickens, but more usually they scavenge dead carcasses or raid garbage dumps, rather than hunt like wolves.

Life in the home

Unlike wolves, domesticated dogs do not live in packs. However, a dog might consider its owners to be similar to pack leaders. They take the place of the parent wolves.

Dogs will roll on their backs, exposing their stomachs to let you rub or tickle them. They might also nuzzle or lick a person's face. This is the way a passive wolf behaves when it encounters a more assertive wolf.

When tired, a dog might scrape the carpet and circle the spot several times before lying down. Wolves do this when they prepare a place on the ground to settle down for the night.

Common confusions

Smiling dogs

The human smile usually means someone is pleased to see you, but smiling animals may mean something very different. An angry dog pulls back its lips to expose its teeth. It may look as if it is smiling, but it is showing **aggression** and might attack. This is **body language** that can be traced back to its ancestor, the wolf.

The action of your dog licking your face is a throwback to the behavior of a passive wolf reacting to a more dominant one.

Animal welfare

By understanding the behavior of wild animals, scientists are beginning to help make the lives of their captive or domesticated relatives more comfortable.

It's wild

Some animals need to act out natural behaviors no matter what. Take foraging behavior, for example. Some animals have a need to forage and not only eat, even though food is readily available. Pigs need to root around, pushing their snouts into the earth, to find tasty morsels. Even pigs that live in concrete pens and are fed food pellets still root in and chew straw. Pigs are happy when foraging. Similarly, starlings prefer to search for mealworms rather than eat them out of a bird feeder.

Keeping chickens happy

Chickens in **battery cages** are deprived for all sorts of reasons. Chickens are happier when they have space to roam, scratch, and peck, and to bathe in dust. They also seem happier when they build nests. They do this every day and spend as much time working on an old nest as they do building one from scratch. However, they do not like wide-open spaces. They prefer areas with trees, just as their wild, jungle fowl ancestors did.

Egg-laying chickens are crammed into a battery cage on a poultry farm. They remain there, on average, for an entire year before being slaughtered. Most food industry chickens are raised like this.

Very comfortable, thank you!

Some animals do not need to act out natural behaviors if appropriate substitutes are available. Take pregnant pigs, for example. Wild sows (female pigs) that are about to give birth build nests of dried vegetation. Domestic sows do the same with straw provided by the farmer.

However, domestic sows that are given large waterbeds are content to stop nest building and give birth on the waterbed instead. The comfort of the nest is more important than the nest-building behavior. So sows may not suffer because they cannot build a nest, as long as they have a comfortable place to give birth and **suckle** their young.

All this shows how the study of animal behavior is just as important for the welfare of captive and domestic animals as it is for the conservation of animals in the wild.

Domestic pigs like to forage, but, as long as they have comfortable living conditions, they do not feel the need to make a nest.

How Do I Behave?

Human behavior is very complex, and it changes at different times in our lives—unborn baby, infancy, childhood, adolescence, and adulthood. For now, let's look at some of the less complicated forms of our behavior that we can observe. Here are some examples:

Instinct

In the past, scientists thought that only nonhuman animals were guided by instincts (see page 6). Now we know that humans also show instinctive behavior. Closing our eyes when something flashes towards us and quickly withdrawing our hand if we touch a hot saucepan are "behavioral reflexes". The reflex is one of the simplest forms of behavior. Can you think of any more examples?

Hanging on

When a newborn baby grasps a rope or a finger and is lifted up, it will not let go. The baby instinctively holds on tightly. It is probably a throwback to prehistoric times and our **primate** ancestors. Most primates are always on the move to find food, so babies have to hang on tightly to their mothers. A baby automatically holds its mother's fur so it does not fall off when she moves. Human babies have kept this behavior.

Body language

We communicate unknowingly with **body language** (see pages 20–21) through our eye movements, body postures, hand movements, gestures, and facial expressions. However, these can sometimes be confusing. In the Western world, for example, people who maintain eye contact appear to be confident and trustworthy. Those who look away a lot are thought to be less at ease. In parts of Asia, however, looking someone in the eye can be rude. So, making eye contact can cause misunderstandings between people from different backgrounds.

Questions to think about

The position of the eyebrows and mouth on the human face tells others whether you are happy or sad, without the need for words. Can you think of other examples of body language or facial expressions? Do our bodies give our true feelings away?

Living together

Humans are generally social animals. We band together as married couples or partners, families, friends, associations, clubs, tribes, clans, states, and nations. We get together to help one another and to protect each other. This probably follows from our prehistoric past when our primate ancestors formed hunting groups to kill more game. More people in the group can protect both the group and us.

Past, present, and future

Our prehistoric ancestors only considered the present. They did not plan for the future or remember the past. The difference over the past 200,000 years, since modern man **evolved**, is that humans can communicate about events that happened in the past and about what might happen in the future. It is one thing that makes us human.

Mysterious behavior

While scientists are beginning to understand the underlying reasons for many of our everyday behaviors, there are some that are still mysterious.

Questions to think about

Grocery shopping is one way modern humans use our ability to think about the past, present, and future. We buy food in the present, based on food we have eaten in the past, and we store it for the future. Can you think of some more examples?

Blushing

Why do we blush? After all, if we tell a lie, cheat, or are embarrassed, a blush is a dead giveaway. Nobody quite knows why we do it. But whatever the answer, women blush more than men.

Laughter

Why do we laugh? Apparently, when we laugh our bodies produce mood-improving chemicals called endorphins. However, research has shown that we laugh more at fairly ordinary comments than at hilarious jokes. Maybe our laughter has become a social behavior that strengthens the relationships between people.

People laugh, perhaps, in order to bond with other people.

Kissing

Why do we kiss? Is it a memory of breastfeeding when we were infants? Ancient people **weaned** babies from breast milk by feeding them chewed food from the mouth, as chimpanzee mothers do today. Is there a link?

Teenagers

Most animals, including the great apes, move relatively smoothly from childhood to adulthood. Humans spend a decade as teenagers, often struggling against authority. Why? Whatever the answer, prolonged adolescence in humans evolved between 800,000 and 300,000 years ago, not long after a sudden increase in brain size. There also appears to be a reorganization of the brain during the teenaged years. It probably helps the mind deal with the complex social backdrop of modern human life. This makes us different from all other animals.

Rock art

Another human mystery is art. Why do we create images of things around us? Was it originally a way to impress a potential partner, like a peacock's colorful tail? Was it a kind of "social glue" that bonded our ancestors to their families and to tribal groups? What do you think?

The clothes we choose to wear are part of our body language.

Animal Behavior Timeline

2nd century BCE   The Greek **philosopher** Aristotle writes about animal behavior, including an observation that foraging honeybees appear to communicate within the nest.

1775 CE   German theologian and beekeeper Johann Ernst Spitzner (1731–1805) describes dancing in bees.

1861   English naturalist Henry Walter Bates (1825–1892) is first to publish a scientific account of mimicry in animals. He goes to the Amazon rainforest with Alfred Lord Wallace and comes back with over 14,000 **species**, 8,000 of which are new to science.

1872   English naturalist Charles Darwin (1809–1882) writes *The Expressions of Emotions in Man and Animals*. He describes the physical signs of human emotions, such as grimacing (making faces), and shows that they are similar to those in animals, especially domestic dogs and cats and even apes and monkeys. Some scientists consider Darwin to be the first ethologist (scientist who studies animal behavior).

1872   English **biologist** Douglas Spalding (1841–1877) discovers imprinting behavior (which he calls "stamping in") in chickens. This is later studied and popularized by Konrad Lorenz. Some scientists recognize Spalding as the founding father of ethology.

German biologist Oskar Heinroth (1871–1945) rediscovers imprinting many years after Spalding. Some scientists suggest Heinroth is the real founding father of ethology.

1901   Russian physiologist Ivan Pavlov (1849–1936) notices that dogs salivate when he rings a bell before he feeds them, and so he demonstrates the "conditioned reflex."

1923   Karl Ritter von Frisch (1886–1982) publishes his first paper on the language of bees. He studies the way bees perceive the world and communicate, and especially how bees tell others in their hive about distant sources of food by performing a "waggle-dance." In 1973, he shares the Nobel Prize with Lorenz and Tinbergen.

1935   Konrad Lorenz (1903–1989) publishes his studies on imprinting in geese, especially the way goslings adopt as their "mother" the first thing they see when they hatch. They then follow it everywhere. The goslings Lorenz studies even imprint on his boots because they are the very first things the birds see when they come out of their eggs. In 1973, he shares the Nobel Prize with Frisch and Tinbergen.

1944   American researchers Donald Griffin (1915–2003) and Robert Galambos (1914–2010) identify animal echolocation while studying bats. In 1978, Griffin becomes a pioneer of cognitive ethology or "animal thinking."

1951   Nikolaas Tinbergen (1907–1988) publishes his book *The Study of Instinct*. His research focuses on "supernormal stimuli," such as the way a **territorial** male stickleback will attack a wooden fish shape rather than a real male fish if the wood model has a brighter red belly. In 1973, he shares the Nobel Prize with Lorenz and Frisch.

1953   Kinji Imanishi (1902–1992) and Syunzo Kawamura study Japanese macaques and observe the way a female washes potatoes before eating them and how the younger members of the troop soon learn the behavior by copying her.

1965   Jane Morris Goodall writes her first paper on the Gombe chimpanzee. This is her thesis for a PhD in Ethology at Cambridge University, and it covers her first five years studying the Gombe chimpanzees.

1968   Nikolaas Tinbergen collaborates with filmmaker Hugh Falkus on a BBC wildlife film *Signals of Survival*, one of the first films to feature the scientific study of animal behavior.

1970   Gordon G. Gallup, Jr. develops the mirror test to find out whether animals are self-aware and discovers that captive chimpanzees can recognize themselves in a mirror.

1971   Biruté Galdikas begins her research on the behavior and ecology of the orangutans of Borneo. Along with Jane Goodall's study of chimpanzees in Africa, it is one of the longest running studies of a wild **mammal**.

1979   American researcher Francine "Penny" Patterson teaches a modified form of American Sign Language (ASL) to two captive lowland gorillas.

1983   Dian Fossey (1932–1985) publishes her book *Gorillas in the Mist* about her work studying the behavior of mountain gorillas in Rwanda. A feature film of the same name, starring Sigourney Weaver, is released in 1988. Dian is tragically killed by poachers in 1985.

1990   David Attenborough presents *The Trials of Life*, a wildlife documentary that explores animal behavior and the way animals face up to their journey through life from birth to death. This is the third of his major landmark series – the first two were *Life on Earth* (1979) about evolution, and *Living Planet* (1984) about ecology.

2002   Alex Kacelnik, Professor of Behavioral Ecology at Oxford University, reveals that a crow called Betty is able to make and use tools out pieces of metal.

Glossary

aggression intending or threatening to cause harm to a member of the same or other species

anxiety feelings of fear, worry, and uneasiness

assertive bold or confident

bacteria single-celled microorganisms with no distinct nucleus. Bacteria are the most abundant life forms on Earth.

bait use food as a bait to entice animals to come closer or to catch them

battery cage type of cage used in intense poultry farming, in which chickens are kept indoors in small cages in order to raise more of them cheaply. Sixty percent of the world's eggs are produced this way. Battery cages have been illegal in the European Union since 2012.

biologist person who studies living things

body language conscious or unconscious movements of the body that can communicate an animal's or person's feelings

brood number of young born or hatched at the same time

cannibalism eating members of your own species

courtship ritual to select a mate or partner

dilate get bigger or expand

domesticated tamed to live alongside people—to be fed, watered, and controlled by people

dominant exercising the most influence or control

environment living and non-living surroundings of an individual

enzyme special chemical (protein) that helps chemical changes take place in living organisms

evolve to develop gradually by the process of evolution. Evolution is the gradual change of characteristics of a population of living things from one generation to the next.

exoskeleton hard outer "skin" of insects, spiders, crabs, and lobsters

feral wild. Domesticated animals or pets may go back to living as feral animals.

forage search for food

gene means by which the blueprint for a living thing's appearance and instinctive behavior is passed from parent to offspring

habituate get used to something

imitate copy the behavior of others

infanticide killing infants or children

invertebrate animal without a backbone

mammal member of a group of animals with hair or fur that produce milk to feed their offspring

migrate go on a journey, often between winter feeding and summer breeding sites

modify change in form or character

mourn express grief or sorrow for the dead

mystical mysterious and beyond normal senses

nutrient chemical an organism needs to live and grow

organism living thing

optimist someone who usually expects the best to happen in any situation

orient find one's position

passive inactive, submissive, or not resisting

pessimist someone who usually expects the worst to happen in any situation

philosopher person who studies the nature of knowledge and existence

predator animal that catches other animals for food

prey animals that are caught for food

primate member of a group of mammals with grasping hands and feet, nails, a short snout, eyes facing forward, and a large brain

reasoning figuring things out

regurgitate bring up food from the stomach

resemblance similarity

ritual pattern of behavior performed regularly in a set manner

society group of individuals that are dependent on one another

species living organisms able to breed with each other

stamina able to keep going no matter what

stimulus something that causes an organism to respond

submissive giving in to the will of another

suckle feed young mammals with milk from their mother's body

territory living space defended by an animal or group of animals

undulating wavy motion

vegetarian person or animal that does not eat other animals or meat

wean change a mammal infant's diet from mother's milk to solid food

zoologist person who studies animals

Find Out More

Books

Bright, Michael. *The Diversity of Species* (Timeline: Life on Earth series). Chicago, IL: Heinemann Library, 2009.

Bright, Michael. *Extinctions of Living Things* (Timeline: Life on Earth series). Chicago, IL: Heinemann Library, 2009.

Hartman, Eve and Wendy Meshbesher. *Changing Life on Earth*. Chicago, IL: Raintree, 2009.

Haugen, Brenda. *Jane Goodall: Legendary Primatologist*. Mankato, MN: Compass Point Books, 2006.

Moore, Heidi. *Dian Fossey*. Chicago, IL: Raintree, 2009.

Nardo, Don. *The Theory of Evolution: A History of Life on Earth*. Mankato, MN: Compass Point Books, 2010.

Websites

www.bbc.co.uk/nature
BBC Nature: Learn about the world of nature from the BBC here.

www.bbc.co.uk/wildlifefinder
The BBC Wildlife Finder has lots of information and videos on wildlife.

www.discoverwildlife.com
The BBC Wildlife magazine has lots of information on wildlife worldwide.

www.nationalgeographic.com
The National Geographic Society website has more information about wildlife and animal behavior.

www.amnh.org
Explore the natural world at the American Museum of Natural History website.

www.guardian.co.uk/science/animalbehaviour
This *Guardian* newspaper website has information on animal behavior.

kids.nationalgeographic.com/kids/animals
This National Geographic site for kids features the world's fascinating animals.

www.arkive.org
Arkive is a website with information, stills, and video images of endangered species (from the world's leading wildlife photographers and filmmakers).

www.seaworld.org/animal-info/animal-bytes
The Animal Bytes website has information on selected animals.

animal.discovery.com
The Animal Planet website has lots of information about the behavior of wild animals and pets.

news.bbc.co.uk/1/hi/sci/tech/8029977.stm
On this website you can watch Betty the clever crow in action!

users.ox.ac.uk/~kgroup/tools/introduction.shtml
Learn more about Oxford University's research into Betty the crow on this website.

www.lascaux.culture.fr
Virtually visit the astounding Lascaux cave paintings in France (look for the English language button on the sidebar).

DVDs/Blue-ray

Life (2009)

The BBC Natural History Unit series about the innovative, intelligent, and sometimes amazing tactics animals and plants use in order to survive. Narrated by David Attenborough.

The Trials of Life (1990)

The classic BBC Natural History Unit series that examines animal behavior in all its infinite variety. Presented by David Attenborough.

Topics to research

Communication
See what you can find out about people trying to communicate directly with animals using human sign languages, the English language itself, and other means, such as computers, touch screens, and different-shaped objects. There have been experiments with gorillas, chimpanzees, bonobos, orangutans, parrots, and dolphins. Which animals do you think respond to these experiments best, and what do you think it tells us about their intelligence? Look out for Koko, Tanzi, and Alex.

Echolocation
Investigate echolocation behavior. Which animals echolocate to find their way around, and how do they do it? You've probably heard about echolocation in bats, dolphins, and killer whales, but what about fruit bats, seals, shrews, tenrecs, oilbirds, and swiftlets? Further, do we use echolocation? For example, a blind person might tap his or her cane to understand the surroundings. Also explore the following: James Holman, Daniel Kish, Ben Underwood, and Lawrence Scadden. See what you find out!

Index